D1201070

Machines in Motion

MILITARY MACHINES

By Jessica Cohn

Gareth Stevens
Publishing

Please visit our website, www.garethstevens.com. For a free color catalog of all our high-quality books, call toll free 1-800-542-2595 or fax 1-877-542-2596.

Library of Congress Cataloging-in-Publication Data

Cohn, Jessica.
Military machines / by Jessica Cohn.
  p. cm. — (Machines in motion)
Includes index.
ISBN 978-1-4339-9605-4 (pbk.)
ISBN 978-1-4339-9606-1 (6-pack)
ISBN 978-1-4339-9604-7 (library binding)
1. Military weapons—Juvenile literature. 2. Vehicles, Military—Juvenile literature. 3. Airplanes, Military—Juvenile literature. 4. Warships—Juvenile literature. I. Cohn, Jessica. II. Title.
UF500.C64 2014
623.4—dc23

First Edition
Published in 2014 by
Gareth Stevens Publishing
111 East 14th Street, Suite 349
New York, NY 10003

©2013 Gareth Stevens Publishing

Produced by Netscribes Inc.
Art Director Dibakar Acharjee
Editorial Content Jessica Cohn
Copy Editor Dorothy Anderson
Picture Researcher Sandeep Kumar G
Designer Rishi Raj
Illustrators Ashish Tanwar, Indranil Ganguly, Prithwiraj Samat, and Rohit Sharma

Photo credits:
Page no. = #, t = top, a = above, b = below, l = left, r = right, c = center
Front Cover: Shutterstock Images LLC Title Page: Shutterstock Images LLC
Contents Page: Shutterstock Images LLC Inside: Netscribes Inc.: 15b, 42, 43 Shutterstock Images LLC: 5t, 6, 7t, 7b, 9, 11t, 11b, 12, 13, 14, 17, 21t, 21b, 21c, 25t, 25b, 27b, 32, 34, 35, 37t, 37b, 39, 40 Military photos courtesy of the U.S. Department of Defense: 4, 5b, 8, 10, 15t, 16, 19, 20, 22, 24, 26, 27t, 28t, 28b, 29, 30, 31, 33t, 36, 38, 41 NASA: 18.

Printed in the United States of America

CPSIA compliance information: Batch #CS13GS: For further information contact Gareth Stevens, New York, New York at 1-800-542-2595.

Contents

MILITARY MIGHT

In war, nothing is more important than the soldiers who risk their lives, but the troops must have guns and other weapons. The armed forces rely on war machines to move their supplies. They need many machines to help them fight.

What do you know about these military machines?

Land, Air, and Sea

Tanks help troops fight battles on land. These powerful war machines have **armor** to protect the people inside. The military also has fighter jets. The troops who protect the U.S. coasts use ships also built with long-range weapons.

In this book, you will look closely at military **vehicles** used on land, in the air, and at sea. You will discover what makes them mighty.

TANKS

Tanks can roll over mud, sand, and rocks. These mighty machines are armed and armored. They can power their way through firefights. The bullets shot from small guns bounce off their sides.

The first tanks appeared during World War I (1914–1918). Back then, the name for these vehicles was landships. The landships moved on wheels that turned long **tracks**. The tracks could run over the long **trenches** dug in the ground.

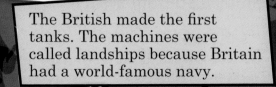

The British made the first tanks. The machines were called landships because Britain had a world-famous navy.

The United States fought alongside Great Britain, France, Russia, and other nations. They fought together against Germany and Austria-Hungary, among others.

Digging in

People called World War I the "war to end all wars." Many nations sent troops to Europe. The fighting was fierce. For the first time, the soldiers fought with machine guns.

In some places, the soldiers dug trenches so they could stay below the shooting. Tanks helped with this new kind of fighting. The military made the machines for trench warfare.

Weighty Matter

Over time, the U.S. armed forces built many models of these tough war machines. They loaded U.S. tanks with powerful **munitions**.

Today, military tanks are often sorted by the time they were built. They can also be divided by their weights.

The first U.S. tanks were top secret! The workers who built them thought the vehicles would carry water, and that is how tanks got their name. The military shipped the machines in wooden boxes. The boxes were labeled "tank," as in "water tank."

The Pershing was made for World War II (1939–1945). The United States, Britain, and other nations fought against Germany, Italy, and Japan.

The M46 Patton was named for U.S. General George Patton. He was a general during World War II.

Going Lighter

To fight in World War II, the United States made the M26. Officials also called this war machine the Pershing. John Pershing was a U.S. general during World War I.

After World War II, tanks like the M46 appeared. It was a medium tank. Light tanks arrived in the 1960s. They were able to move faster than heavier tanks. They were also easier to load into planes so they could be flown from place to place.

Ready for War

Modern tanks are built to fight other tanks. They have to withstand terrible firefights. They also must be able to go long distances, so they need to be able to hold lots of **fuel**. These important war machines need plenty of power. They have to climb hills and speed up as needed.

A tank's weight is measured in pounds or kilograms, but the power of the engine is measured in **horsepower**. Both measures help decide how fast the vehicle can go.

The original M1 Abrams was named for U.S. General Creighton Abrams. He was a general in the Vietnam War, which lasted from 1957 to 1975. The M1 series has gone through several upgrades.

The M1 series is fitted with engines that provide 1,500 horsepower. Strong people can sometimes deliver 1 horsepower, but most people who lift or move things produce a small part of 1 horsepower.

⚡ POWER ON

Long ago, a man named James Watt figured out what one horse could raise on a **pulley**. He found that one horse could raise 330 pounds of coal 100 feet in one minute. You can multiply those numbers to see why 1 horsepower equals 33,000 foot-pounds.

330 x 100 = 33,000

FOUR-BY-FOURS

Like the tank, the jeep is a military classic. The jeep is a 4 x 4. This means all four wheels get power from the engine. The first number in 4 x 4 stands for the number of wheels. The second number tells you the number of wheels the engine powers.

The powered wheels get **torque** from the engine. Torque can be thought of as a turning force. A regular car is often a 4 x 2, but military machines need more force.

In the military, jeeps were marked with the letters *GP*. The letters stood for "General Purpose." The soldiers said or read "*GP*" as "jeep."

The name Humvee comes from the letters the military first used to mark it. Those letters are HMMWV, which stand for "High Mobility Multipurpose Wheeled Vehicle."

Going Wide

The Humvee carries troops in today's war zones. This vehicle is another classic 4 x 4. It is open like the jeep, but it is wider, so it doesn't tip as easily.

The jeep and Humvee are just two of many vehicles the military owns. Both of these war machines run on four wheels. Many others have six or eight wheels.

SIX AND EIGHT WHEELS

The Buffalo H has six wheels and a V-shaped **hull**. This shape helps it withstand explosions. The front is made to cut through flying objects. The Buffalo H can also roll over without hurting the people inside.

The M1127 has eight wheels. This vehicle can run on hard roads or soft surfaces. It has built-in guns to protect the soldiers inside. Its flat top can carry things from one place to another.

The troops inside the Buffalo H wear straps like those used by race car drivers.

The M1127 is also called the Stryker. It can run as an 8 x 4 or as an 8 x 8 when needed.

⚡ POWER ON

An axle is a pin or bar on which a wheel turns. On a motor vehicle, the force that turns the axle comes from the engine. A force is a push or a pull, and a turning force is a twist. On a vehicle, a turning force rotates the axle, which turns the wheels.

Try turning a doorknob slowly and thinking about what is happening. Whenever you turn a doorknob, you are making a turning force. The knob is like a wheel, and the shaft of the doorknob is like an axle.

SCOUTING VEHICLES

Troops use the M1127 for scouting. It has the right features for this important job. Scouting machines need armor and weapons because they draw fire. Yet they also need to be lightweight so they can move fast.

Surveillance means gathering information. It is another word for scouting. The M1127 is just one kind of scout vehicle. A new family of scout vehicles called the Cougars is equipped to meet all kinds of challenges.

The Cougars are scout vehicles. Some are 4 x 4s. Others are 6 x 6s.

Gone Scouting

Scout vehicles operate in many conditions. Many work well on sand, but they can also go through high water. Some of these machines can travel hundreds of miles without stopping.

Today's war machines are like the grandchildren of the World War II scout vehicles. The early spy vehicles included the M3A1. It had room for seven people, and it could even carry wounded soldiers. Then as now, each scout vehicle had many jobs to do.

The M3A1s had machine guns on them. Older vehicles like the M3A1s are used as long as they keep working.

Supersecret

The U.S. military is trying out new scout vehicles. Many of the new machines are UGVs. The letters stand for "Unmanned Ground Vehicles." This means they run without people aboard.

UGVs are more like **robots** than vehicles. The troops operate these machines from a distance. They work much like **remote control** cars. The UGVs work well in dangerous situations. For example, some of the machines have equipment that can stop a bomb from going off.

The United States has been making UGVs for jobs in space, too. The *Curiosity* rover explores Mars.

Out of Control

The U.S. Army is also working on war machines, called drones, that need no operator. The machines run themselves. They have special **sensors** that can figure out what is going on around them.

Machines with sensors can go inside buildings to collect information. They can help map what rooms are like. In some cases, the machines can even repair themselves when something breaks.

The Dragon Runner is a robot with a camera. Troops can carry it and throw it where it needs to go.

ARTILLERY

The **artillery** is the branch of the military that uses guns. Today's troops carry powerful weapons, and they tow large guns behind trucks. The troops travel in vehicles with powerful guns built in.

Troops have machines powerful enough to shoot down airplanes. They use guns that can shoot at planes over long distances. The military calls these machines **antiaircraft systems**. They are among the most powerful weapons on Earth.

The Paladin carries a Howitzer. This type of weapon can aim rockets at distant targets.

March of Time

1 Long ago, weapons were very basic. They shot arrows or rocks and other heavy objects.

2 By the 15th century, cannons were the main artillery. Cannons operated like very heavy guns. They fired solid shots called cannonballs.

3 Over time, many weapons became smaller and more deadly. But modern artillery also includes large long-range rockets and exploding shells.

AIR FORCES

The DPV Fast Attack can travel 80 miles (129 km) per hour, making it one of the fastest war vehicles used on land. But the flying forces of the military travel in the fastest vehicles of all.

Pilots dart through the sky in war machines that can go more than 1,000 miles (1,609 km) an hour. Fighters are the jets built to fire on other planes. Attack aircraft are the airplanes that go after targets on the ground.

The DPV Fast Attack is used by the military's Special Forces.

The U.S. military uses the C-17 for cargo.

Fixed Fascination

Most military aircraft have fixed wings. This means the wings stay in place on the bodies of most of the aircraft. Most also have jet engines, which suck in air from the front. The engines press on the air and then spray fuel on it. They light the materials on fire, and burning gases spray from the back. This pushes the plane forward.

The military also has planes to carry troops and **cargo**. The cargo planes are often easy to spot. They are usually wider than fighters and other superfast aircraft.

Workhorse of the Air

Helicopters have **rotor** blades that spin above the aircraft. The spinning motion allows a helicopter to fly straight up and down, making it possible to get into spaces where a jet could never land.

Among the active helicopters is the HH-60 Pave Hawk. It can help rescue troops who have been left behind in battle.

Double Chin

The CH-47 Chinook can travel 196 miles per hour. This heavy helicopter moves troops, artillery, and other supplies. Its back end has a wide loading ramp. On the bottom, the Chinook has big hooks. It can lift large containers with the hooks.

The hardworking CH-47 Chinook has two lifts. The lifts are the parts with blades that lift the machine off the ground.

POWER ON

Wings and rotors work with air pressure to help move a vehicle through air. To see air pressure in action, fold a piece of paper in half, like a tent. Set the tent on a table, near the edge.

Next, blow softly into one of the open ends of the tent. Your breath lowers the air pressure inside, the paper flattens.

The tent stays standing when the air pressure inside and outside is the same. The tent falls when the air pressure above it becomes heavier than the air pressure below it.

SPACE VEHICLES

The F-22 Raptor is a mighty machine. This superfast fighter can fly 50,000 feet in the air. That is higher than most clouds. Yet some war machines go even faster and higher.

Space is the area 50 miles beyond Earth. Some war machines can reach that mark and go much farther. Among these mighty machines is the Atlas family of rockets. There is also a line of space machines called Delta.

The United States is working with other countries to develop the new launch vehicles.

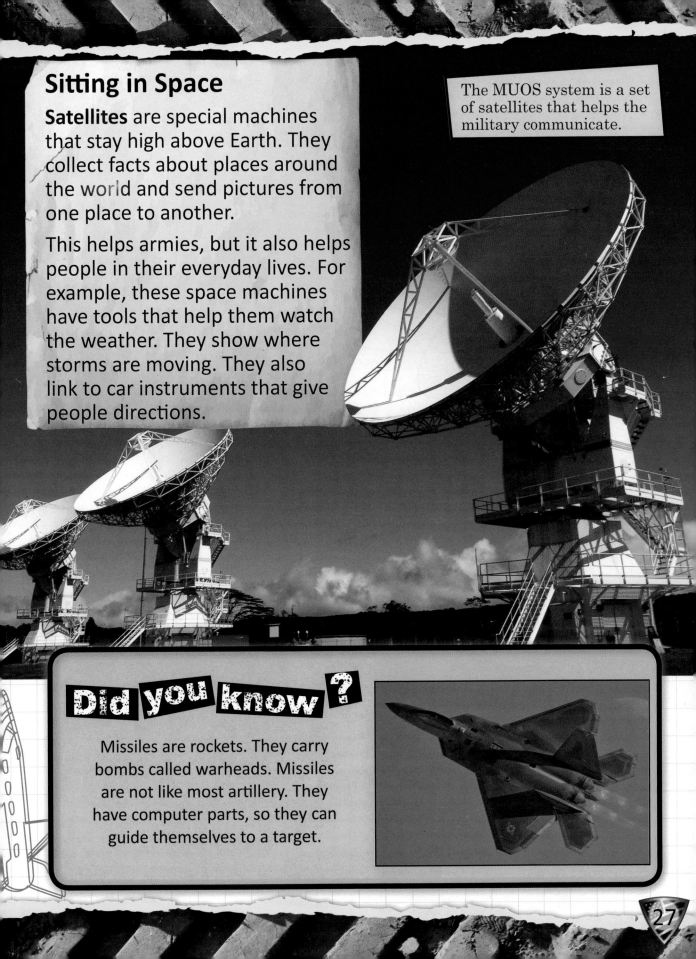

Sitting in Space

Satellites are special machines that stay high above Earth. They collect facts about places around the world and send pictures from one place to another.

This helps armies, but it also helps people in their everyday lives. For example, these space machines have tools that help them watch the weather. They show where storms are moving. They also link to car instruments that give people directions.

The MUOS system is a set of satellites that helps the military communicate.

Did you know?

Missiles are rockets. They carry bombs called warheads. Missiles are not like most artillery. They have computer parts, so they can guide themselves to a target.

SHIPS AND CARRIERS

The United States has to be ready to fight at sea, so ships and boats of many sizes patrol the waters around the world. Among the biggest of the ships are aircraft carriers. The largest of all are called supercarriers.

Aircraft carriers are like floating airports. They can carry many jets. These ships have huge decks. They are long enough and wide enough that the planes can take off and land on top.

The Iowa battleships fought in wars from 1940 to the 1990s. Now, they are being used as museums.

Very few nations of the world have aircraft carriers. These ships are costly to build—and to keep and protect.

Zumwalt destroyers are a new class of ship being made by the U.S. Navy.

Seen at Sea

The U.S. Navy, Army, and Marines all have ships built for battle. Each of these branches of the military has battleships and battle cruisers with powerful guns. The battleships are the larger of the two. They also have heavier armor.

Destroyers are ships that help other ships get across the seas safely. They protect supply ships in dangerous waters. Smaller boats called patrol boats keep watch along the coasts.

SUBMARINES AND SUPPORT SHIPS

Submarines operate underwater. From beneath the waves, they look for ships and other kinds of movement. The large ones carry powerful weapons. They can stay underwater for as long as a half year.

Some of the underwater vehicles are small. They can stay out for just a few hours. Other small machines go out without people aboard. They study what is happening underwater. They send back pictures and other kinds of reports.

Trident submarines carry missiles. They stay below water for many weeks at a time.

A variety of ships is ready for battle at all times in the oceans.

Supporting Role

Many other kinds of ships support warships. For example, supply ships move fuel and other supplies away from land. Fast combat support ships work as go-betweens. They pick up supplies from supply ships, then take the supplies to carriers.

UNTIL NOW

The map shows some of the places around the world where the United States has gone to battle. The most recent U.S. wars and battles have featured new vehicles with high-tech computer parts. Computers are making both the engines and the weapons more advanced. The new land, sea, and air vehicles have equipment that allows them to find their way without maps. Some of the newest weapons are smart bombs. They can hit a target without damaging what is around them.

Bay of Pigs (1961)

Grenada (1983)

Panama (1989)

WWI (1914–1918)

WWII (1939–1945)

Iraq (2003–2011)

Korean War
(1950–1953)

Afghanistan
(2001–present)

Bosnia and
Herzegovina
(1992–1995)

Vietnam War
(1957–1975)

Persian Gulf War
(1990–1991)

IN THE FUTURE

The military is often the first to study ideas that seem out-of-this-world. Right now, researchers are experimenting with machines that are small and low to the ground. This will make it hard for others to see them. Some of the new instruments will have special coatings. The coatings make it hard for **radar** to find them.

The military uses computers to test ideas before building the vehicles.

Robot Army

The U.S. Army is making machines that work like insects. The RHex has six legs that allow it to jump around. It moves on sand the way a sand bug does. The military has also been developing drones that can stop bombs from going off.

The new robots have hands that can carry dangerous items.

New to the Scene

The U.S. Air Force and other branches of the military worked for many years on the F-35 Joint Strike Fighter. This super jet flies really fast, but is can also stop in the air, go up and down, and move backward!

The military has also been working on space vehicles that look like a cross between a jet and a rocket. Most of these plans are top secret, but it is clear that the new planes will go farther into space than regular jets ever could.

The parts of the F-35 have been tested thousands of times in recent years.

The military puts on air shows to show people the tricks jets can do.

Did you know?

Each year, U.S. car companies put on shows of their new models. People from all over attend the shows to see the exciting new ideas in action. The military has similar shows. Engineers work on new models and then take them out for others to see. They use the feedback to make any necessary changes.

Mix and Match

The U.S. military has several branches. They all study the ways that war changes over time. Then they each build machines to meet their new needs.

Today, U.S. Army officials are building vehicles that work well in deserts and need less maintenance than the vehicles they now have. The U.S. Navy is working on a new submarine with more firepower. It will be able to stay hidden because of its secret features. The Air Force is creating weapons that can be sent from even longer distances than before. Officials are preparing new machines for a mix of challenges.

The Cougars are machines that can do many kinds of jobs and need less maintenance than the vehicles they replaced.

During the planning process, the military starts with models of the new machines.

Ideas in Action

EFVs are a new line of land vehicles. The letters *EFV* stand for "**Expeditionary** Fighting Vehicle." The military is also working on machines called GCVs. These letters stand for "Ground Combat Vehicles." The new vehicles must be able to last in heavy firefights.

Ready for Anything

Engineers are working on machines to succeed the Humvee. The troops need something lighter that does the same job. The military needs vehicles that take less energy to run.

Another line of machines undergoing improvements are the MRAPs. The letters in MRAP stand for "Mine-**Resistant** Ambush Protected." Mines are traps that are set to blow up. An ambush is a surprise attack. Today's troops need machines that can withstand both.

Strike Force

The Stryker is a MRAP often used for scouting. The Stryker can move over sand. It is heavier than most road vehicles, but it is light for a war machine. Planes can carry the Stryker from one place to another.

This war machine operates like a car. The driver simply puts the vehicle in drive.

A camera shows video of what is ahead. The special camera can "see" at night and through dust.

Weapons are built into all sides of the vehicle.

The Stryker reaches speeds of up to 62 miles per hour.

The eight wheels work in off-road settings.

QUICK DRAW

People who plan how vehicles will look have special computer programs that let them draw new concepts. Their drawings show height, width, and depth. But they often start by making drawings on paper. Here is how to draw a tank.

1

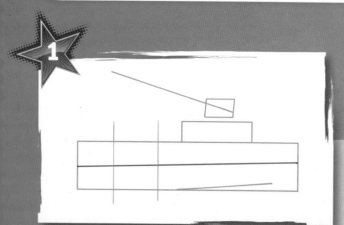

Materials Needed

- Paper, graphing paper optional
- Pencil

Start by making light boxes for the bottom and top of the vehicle. To make a vehicle like the Stryker, you can start with a large, long box for the bottom. Make a smaller box for the cab. Make an even smaller box for the base of the gun.

2

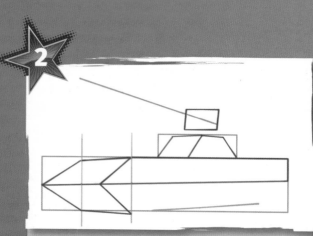

Now, you can start to make lines that better show what the front and cab look like.

3

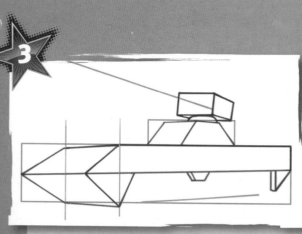

Keep adding lines and details. If you want to be fancy, show a tilt on the base of the gun.

4

For each wheel, draw the largest circle, and then add a curved line at the "front" to show depth. Then, fill in the center.

5

Draw the top line and bottom line of the gun. Join the lines at the "front" with a small circle to show depth. Fill in details one small line at a time.

6

Keep working to add as many details as possible. Do not forget the wheel on the far side.

7

Darken the main lines. Erase the light lines for the boxes that helped you at the start.

Build a Report

Ready to write a book report about *Military Machines*?

A book report explains what you have read so others can understand it, too. Your report should be in paragraph form. A paragraph is a group of sentences that tells something about the same thing. One of the sentences explains the main idea. This is often the first sentence of each paragraph, but it does not have to be.

You can build a report using these steps.

1. Begin with an introduction. Give the name of the book, and be sure to underline the name. Tell the reader what the book is about.

2. Then, explain what you learned by reading. Do not try to explain everything. Just write about one or two main ideas. For this step, you can look at the table of contents at the front of the book. This will remind you what the book covered.

3. Quite often, the conclusion is your opinion about the book. Or it can explain what you learned while reading. You can talk about what the book made you think about for the first time.

Show You Know

See how much you remember from your reading. Here are ten questions. The answers can be found inside the book.

1. What were the first tanks called?
2. Which unit of measurement is used for engine power?
3. What is scouting?
4. What are missiles?
5. Which space vehicles stay in space?
6. What does it mean to have fixed wings?
7. What kind of ship is like a floating airport?
8. Which new robot looks like an insect?
9. What does GCV stand for?
10. Give an example of a MRAP used in desert fighting.

Answers:

1. landships 2. horsepower 3. looking around, or surveillance 4. rockets that carry bombs 5. satellites 6. wings that stay in place 7. aircraft carrier 8. RHex 9. Ground Combat Vehicle 10. Stryker

Glossary

antiaircraft systems machines made to shoot down planes

armor a heavy covering made to protect something

artillery large weapons, especially weapons built into a vehicle; also, the people who operate these weapons

cargo goods carried by vehicles

engineers people who design and build machines

expeditionary of or relating to a journey

fuel a material that produces power when burned

horsepower a unit of measurement for engine power

hull the frame of a heavy vehicle, such as a ship

munitions weapons or arms

pilots people who steer planes, ships, and spacecraft

pulley a rope and wheel structured to pull on and lift things

radar tool that uses radio waves to locate objects

remote control of or related to taking charge of a machine's movement from somewhere apart from the moving machine

resistant able to act against some kind of act, such as movement

robots machines that can perform acts

rotor a machine part that turns all the way around in something else

satellites machines that circle Earth and other large bodies in space

sensors devices that respond to heat or other agents

surveillance close watch kept over someone or something

torque the force that produces turning in a machine

tracks belts that loop around wheels and are turned by the wheels

trenches long cuts dug into the ground

vehicles means of carrying people and things, such as ships, planes, and tanks

For More Information

Books

Allen, Kenny. *Aircraft Carriers (Monster Machines).* Gareth Stevens, 2012.

Hansen, Ole Steen, and Alex Pang. *The F/A-22 Raptor.* Capstone Press, 2006.

Jackson, Kay. *Military Tanks in Action (Amazing Military Vehicles).* PowerKids Press, 2009.

La Padula, Tom. *Learn to Draw Tanks, Aircraft, & Armored Vehicles.* Walter Foster, 2011.

Web Sites

Military Channel

military.discovery.com

The Military Channel offers an online library of videos and a number of related games, covering all branches of the military.

NASA Kid's Page: Engines

grc.nasa.gov/WWW/k-12/UEET/StudentSite/engines.html

NASA answers the question, "How does a jet engine work?"

Smithsonian National Air and Space Museum

airandspace.si.edu/exhibitions/gal104/uav.cfm

Read more about military unmanned aerial vehicles.

Index